WORLD

IS BETTER WITH YOU IN IT!

BELIEVE IN YOURSELF YOU CAN DO IT!

Thank you for choosing our book. It's our priority to continue providing most useful and qualitative books to customers like you. Please leave us a review on Amazon.com. It will only take a minute, but your valuable feedback will help us to get better. Thank you!

♡

SEE MORE BOOKS ON
AMAZON.COM/AUTHOR/HEARTTOHEART

Made in the USA
Coppell, TX
14 December 2021

68582368R00024